More Praise for The As

Brian Orme's *The Ascende*
This is not to say that it's not practically,
it's divinely practical and hits at the core of authentic Christianity. His use of revelation, declaration, and meditation in each day's encounter is a brilliant way of moving the reader from hearing to believing.

Every time I hear Brian speak or read what he writes, I expect my head to hurt, my heart to expand, and my spirit to soar. Reading *The Ascended Life: Volume II* did not disappoint. It's a must-read for all of us who long to live in the reality of the Kingdom and experience all Jesus provided through His life, death, resurrection, and ascension.

David Crone
Senior Leader of The Mission, Vacaville, CA
Author of *Prisoner of Hope, 21 Days of Hope,*
Decisions That Define Us, and more

Brian is an amazing articulator of truth. He takes hidden gems in scripture and unpacks them for us so that they come alive with meaning and purpose. This 21-day truth infusion will take you to a higher and more secure place in God. As you let the truths within these pages penetrate your heart you will be filled with greater hope, joy, and faith. Great job, Brian!

Keith Ferrante
Founder of Emerging Prophets
Author of *The Happy Prophet, There Must Be More,*
Embracing the Emerging Prophets, and more
www.EmergingProphets.com

As for me—a former atheist, now Christian—I can say Brian is truly gifted by God to bring Kingdom truth that is relevant to everyday life. *The Ascended Life: Volume II* shares deep revelations from the storehouse of his personal walk with Christ. I believe Brian Orme has the Matthew 13:52 anointing, bringing old and new treasures as instructed by the Holy Spirit, casting the light of Christ far and wide in a dark world.

Brae Wyckoff
Author of *Demons & Thieves*
Director of Kingdom Writers Association

The Ascended Life: Volume II is a 21-day journey designed to give readers practical insight and revelation to understand our position as believers in Jesus Christ. It is a call to live a life as a co-heir with Jesus and to come into divine health so that the reader steps into ascended living! I love this book because each teaching does not just impart information or truth. Brian takes the reader deeper by opening the way to decree and activate what is being taught. Amazing book!

Shannon Schreyer
Senior Leader of God's Place, Ogden, UT

When you find yourself understanding profound truths and realizing that you have engaged in a process of thinking unlike any other time you have known, then you have found a gem worth keeping. Brian Orme has created that gem with his book *The Ascended Life: Volume II*. He certainly takes you on a journey—a journey you just want to keep on pursuing. This is more than just another book, this is a discovery manual that is practical, challenging, inspiring, and just plain interesting. Brian never ceases to amaze me with his clarity of thought as he sneaks up on you and provides you with yet another insight. I always have something to think about from even just a short conversation with him. This is a man who doesn't just talk about things from a theory position, but also from an experiential position. He walks out what he talks—a rare commodity today. As you discover and embrace profound insights each day you cannot help but be transformed by this book.

Mark Crawford
Founder of Kingdom Development Group
Author of *Fascinated by Heaven on Earth* and *Who Let the Joy Out*

The face of the church is changing. In the framework of that revelation, the relevance and practicality of the message and power of Jesus in the lives of humans are being tested in nearly every way. Brian is addressing and enabling others to practice the "how" of the complicated Christianity of our time. I am so grateful that he exists and that he has written the principles, meditations, and encouragement for today. I wholeheartedly recommend this book to you and your community because the times are changing, and this tool will help you navigate and influence them.

Tommy Green
Founder of Sleeping Giant | Founder of The REV Gatherings

Living with an upgraded perceptive is our inheritance as believers in Christ. This new way of thinking and living that Christ came to demonstrate while He walked the earth is a game changer. Brian Orme once again has written a 21-day revelatory heart map into entering and discovering this upgrade perspective. This book is full of practical truths and powerful declarations that will lead to a deeper and more connected life with God. The Ascended Life: Volume II will challenge you to shed the cocoon of mediocrity and defeated living. Brian's fresh perspective will assist you in the process of transformation and becoming a game changer to the world around you.

Matt Gonzales
Co-Founder of Kingdom Culture Ministries

Brian Orme writes multi-dimensional truths that take your DNA to a Whole. 'Nuthah. Level. They are simple for the children we must become to step into the kingdom and yet deep enough to drown the lies that entangle themselves so subtly into our belief systems. It is powerful to read, declare, and meditate ourselves into wholeness on a daily basis. For all the people who wish they knew how to develop mature beliefs and share them with others, this is Deepness for Dummies! Easy to use, simple to implement, and deeply impactful to the core of your inner self!

Encourage yourself and follow the simple path as Brian's words lead you into ascension through a 21-day adventure of practical and supernatural intimacy development with God.

Eric Waterbury
Founder of World Changers
www.epiclife.org

THE ASCENDED LIFE: VOLUME II

A 21-Day Guidebook to Co-Ascended
Thinking and Breakthrough

Brian Orme

Foreword by Dan McCollam

www.iborme.com

THE ASCENDED LIFE: VOLUME II

A 21-Day Guidebook to Co-Ascended Thinking and Breakthrough

The Ascended Life: Volume II is the follow-up tool that will help elevate your thinking, bring awareness of your co-ascension in Christ, and empower you to live from a higher vantage point.

© Copyright 2018 Brian Orme

www.iborme.com

ISBN 978-0-9977856-3-0

Editor: Elizabeth Chung

Cover Design & Formatting: Brian Orme and Raechel Wong

ACKNOWLEDGEMENTS

First, I want to thank my wife, Cecilee, the most important human in my life. You continue to amaze me with your fierce persistence, clever humor, enduring faith, soft heart, and incredible beauty. There is no one better than you with whom to laugh, cry, or take a leap of faith. I love you.

Thank you to my children, Eowyn and Liam. You both are beyond amazing. The level of creativity, discernment, confidence, humor, and love in which you flow is awe-inspiring. You have changed my world and you'll bring that everywhere you go. I love you.

I would like to honor my parents, Ralph and Mary Jean Orme. I am so grateful to have had parents that stayed together and modeled lives surrendered to Jesus. I am the man I am today because of your faithfulness, compassion, and love for God. I love you, and will see you soon, Dad.

I would like to acknowledge the following people (in no particular order) who have encouraged, challenged, and inspired me to dream big and love deep: Shannon and Nancy Schreyer, Eric Waterbury, Matt Gonzales, Dan McCollam, Banning Liebscher, Shawn Bolz, Dave and Deb Crone, Keith Ferrante, my in-laws Bob and April Basura, and my grandma, Georgia Boynton, who is cheering me on with the cloud of witnesses.

I would like to thank all my spiritual sons and

daughters that God has brought into my life. You all have taught me so much about the Father's love, the fullness of the Kingdom, and the beauty of relationship. I am humbled and honored to be in your lives and watch you change the world.

Lastly, I would like to thank the following heroes in the Body of Christ that have had significant influence in my life: Bill Johnson, Harold Eberle, Jonathan Welton, Georgian and Winnie Banov, Sean Smith, Bobby Conner, and Randy Clark.

CONTENTS

Preface i

Foreword iii

Day 1: Prison of Freedom.. 1

Day 2: Ditching Disappointment................................... 4

Day 3: Cosmic Confrontation 7

Day 4: Before Time | In Time 10

Day 5: Meandering With Purpose 13

Day 6: The Pattern of All Things................................ 16

Day 7: Guardians of the Galaxy................................. 19

Day 8: Kingdom Grounds 22

Day 9: Microscopes and Mirrors 25

Day 10: No Way Is There Gray 28

Day 11: Piercing and Peaceful 31

Day 12: Unity vs. Uniformity 34

Day 13: Multi-Dimensional Space 37

Day 14: The Roars of the Lionesses 40

Day 15: Discipleship 2.0 43

Day 16: The Divine Trine 46

Day 17: The Source Code 49

Day 18: Fruitful Intoxication..................................... 52

Day 19: Settling 55

Day 20: Holy Help... 58

Day 21: The Frequency of Old and New Creation.................. 61

About the Author: 65

PREFACE

We co-exist with Christ in His multi-dimensional world. We are the promised star seed. Just as the stars in the heavens light the earth, we are to be the light of the world. Just as the stars are signs in the heavens, we are to be signs on the earth of heaven. Eternity is not simply in the future, it is now. We have co-ascended with Christ and live as multi-dimensional creations that are in heaven and on earth simultaneously. We are new beings.

We are living in a reality of time-bending possibilities and are infused with supernatural power, wisdom, revelation, and more. This is an expansive world beyond our wildest imaginations. Heaven's design is superimposed upon the earth while we carry an ambassadorial call to release the governing influence of heaven to all spheres of society.

Rise up, new creations. Expand your capacity to dream. Engage your heart to experience all that has been freely given to you and made accessible to you through the finished work of Christ. You are the meeting place of heaven and earth. Don't just know who you are, but also what you are.

The heartbeat of this book is to provoke you to think higher, become more aware of your co-ascension in Christ, and allow your mindsets to be shaped by this reality. In Christ we have the highest point of reference possible. It is called being seated with Christ in the heavenly realms (Ephesians 2:6). We are in Him and He is in us, meandering the trails of life. In Christ we were co-crucified, co-buried, co-resurrected, and we co-ascended.

The Ascended Life: Volume II is a 21-day guidebook to help you see from a higher perspective. Height brings sight. It's a journey towards a mental relocation to throne life realities.

Let's begin to live and function from our co-ascension in Christ. It's a place above the cares and affairs of a world that we are not of. A place from which we can make the greatest impact on the earth. We were made new for this purpose and walking in it will transform how we live today and tomorrow.

FOREWORD

Einstein (a name synonymous with the term "genius") said that a problem cannot be solved with the same mindset that created it. This principle shows us that an ascended lifestyle requires transcendent thinking, or as the author writes in this book, "We need spiritual substance outside of our physical existence." But where can one find such unearthly revelation?

Perhaps the ancient seers could provide an answer. In the time of the prophet Daniel (roughly 620 to 538 B.C.) the young Israelite was found accessing wisdom and knowledge that so far exceeded the current thinking of his day that he was asked for the secret of his source. Daniel replied simply that it is God who is a revealer of secrets. Union with God and a deep spiritual alignment with His word are the pure sources of transcendent thinking. This is the source I have recognized in the life and writing of Brian Orme.

Brian is one of the brilliant emerging voices clothed with a Daniel-like wisdom that is propelling our generation to new heights and depths of spiritual mastery. He has cracked the code of unlocking the deepest of spiritual secrets in a way that is shockingly brief and intellectually accessible, all the while being biblically sound. Brian invites us on a "journey towards a mental relocation to throne life realities."

Notable stops along this journey include the mysteries of multi-dimensional reality, co-creation, time bending, quantum physics, and the "centrifugal force" of free will. Yet, there are also practical rest stops on this road trip dealing with topics as personal as insecurity, self-image, the power of words, and spiritual warfare. At the end of each brief meditation, Brian pens a prayerful declaration of truths that offer the first steps of momentum to propel us from concept to action.

In addition to the genesis of thought I experienced in this book, I am a personal witness to the transformational fruit of Brian's life. I have seen his Christ-centeredness and have observed its impact on his family, friends, and ministry in the real world. It is my confidence in Brian's character, his pursuit of Jesus Christ, and attention to biblical accuracy that have me heartily endorsing and recommending this work.

For some, this second installment of The Ascended Life will be like a fragrant bouquet of brilliant new ideas; for others, it will be a comforting confirmation that their own out-of-the-box thoughts have roots in the ancient biblical record of eternal truth. In either case, you're going to love this fascinating 21-day journey into the ascended life.

Dan McCollam
Director of Sounds of the Nations and the Prophetic Company

DAY 1: PRISON OF FREEDOM

Zechariah 9:12 says, "Return to your stronghold, O prisoners of hope; today I declare that I will restore to you double."

Everyone is a prisoner of something. You can be a prisoner of either fear or hope, darkness or light. The difference is that one is a place of bondage, while the other is a place of freedom. The latter is the paradox of a hope-filled prison. When you are chained to hope, you are free to soar.

Hope secures the soul and anchors it in certainty, just as God is always certain and cannot be anything but steadfast. Unfortunately, we live in a world of incessant anxiety, and technology continues to feed this distress and uneasiness (think social media, for instance).

We become anxious because we don't know. If we knew, we wouldn't be anxious. Thankfully, 1 John

2:20 says, "But you have been anointed by the Holy One, and you all have knowledge." The word "know" here is the Greek word eido, which means "seeing that becomes knowing." This knowing is a gateway that connects the heavenly realms and physical realm. Hope is the ability to see into the heavenly realms and thus know and understand how things truly are.

HOPE IS NOT SIMPLY AN INTELLECTUAL CONCEPT. IT IS REALITY.

To reiterate, we have been anointed to know all things. We don't have to be anxious about anything when we understand we have been anointed to know all things. The Holy Spirit is our guide into reality, the truth. He desires to align our thinking with the stability and constancy of our Father.

Hope is not simply an intellectual concept. It is reality. The fullness of hope—the hope of glory—has been given to us: Jesus Himself.

Hope prisons come with double restoration, according to the verse in Zechariah. God is in the business of restoring all things above and beyond. Our Father doesn't just simply provide; He provides abundantly. Return today to the awareness of the oceans of hope you have been given. Lock yourself up with expectancy and stand on certainty, knowing that things stolen and lost are coming back, two-fold.

Speak Up: Declaration

I declare that I can be anxious about nothing because I have been anointed to know all things. The Holy Spirit's anointing is helping me to remember what I have always known in Christ. I reject anxiety and fully embrace the certainty of knowing. My Father is always stable, so I can be stable in all seasons of life. I choose to lock myself up in hope and sink into expectancy. As I do this, double restoration flows in my direction. Disappointment is not my lover. I have been made one with only One. Jesus, you're my love, my life, and my hope. I declare a double restoration is coming to my life in light of all the things that have been lost or stolen.

Think Deep: Meditation

Zechariah 9:12, 1 John 2:20, Colossians 1:27

DAY 2: DITCHING DISAPPOINTMENT

There are typically two types of disappointed people. The first type wears it on their sleeve and brings up their dissatisfactions in every conversation. The second refuses to acknowledge any disappointment and romanticizes their life into something it is not.

In both cases, the individual has forged a relationship with disappointment. While everyone experiences disappointments in life, some will build a relationship with it that causes them to constantly be weary and shortsighted. Their focus on agreement with the lie increases its influence on their lives. Think of it like this: when a lie is singing a solo, it isn't powerful. We empower it when we begin to join in on the song to make it a duet.

Once we start harmonizing, an energetic and emotional bond forms and twists around a mindset.

Our thought life, and where we focus our attention, can attract the demonic because our thoughts are energetic, and the demonic world needs to feed off of this energy in order to have influence in the physical. Darkness cannot exist in and of itself in the physical world without first being attracted to exist. This happens through agreement.

When we couple with disappointment, it's like we're holding hands with it and walking along the shores of limitation and suppression together, singing off-key in dissonance. As we progress down this path, we then use the past as a frame of reference for how we perceive reality. Ironically, what we're actually perceiving is a virtual reality, a world that's not grounded in truth.

> **WHAT WE SEEK DETERMINES WHAT WE FIND. OUR EXPECTATION DEFINES THE MEASURE OF OUR RECEPTION.**

If we linger here, this will lead to hope deferred, which affects our ability to see in the heavenly realms. Hope is the ability to see clearly. Proverbs 11:27 states that when we pursue good, favor will find us. What we seek determines what we find. Our expectation will define the measure of our reception. Whoever has the greatest awareness of hope will have the greatest awareness of the heavenly realms.

What are we paying attention to? Have we been singing a discordant duet?

Speak Up: Declaration

I decree that I break off my relationship with disappointment. I will no longer romanticize my life as something it is not. Honesty and transparency are the hinges of the door to my breakthrough. I break agreement with every lie that has sought to restrict, constrict, suppress, compress, depress, and shut me down. My pursuit will be of everything good; thus, favor is flowing my direction. My expectancy is tied to my reception. I have hope, so I can see clearly. I say let there be light over my thoughts and that my mind will be filled with clarity.

Think Deep: Meditation

Proverbs 11:27, Ephesians 1:18, Hebrews 11:1

DAY 3: COSMIC CONFRONTATION

When Jesus said in Matthew 16:18, "On this rock I will build my church, and the gates of Hades (underworld) will not prevail," it's important to understand the location of where this conversation took place.

Jesus was in Caesarea Philippi, which was a Roman city located at the base of Mount Hermon, the tallest peak in Israel. The people here worshipped the Greek god Pan. In Genesis 6:1-4, we read that the "sons of God" came down, made an oath, and took and impregnated women, thus producing the Nephilim. According to the Book of Enoch, which calls the fallen angels "watchers," this occurred at the top of Mount Hermon. The Book of Enoch is material that can aid in our study of scripture but wouldn't be considered on the same level with scripture. This

> WE ARE SEATED WITH CHRIST ABOVE, PARTNERING WITH HIM TO EXTEND THE KINGDOM OF ORDER WITHIN A WORLD OF DISORDER.

book helps shed some light on what took place in Genesis 6.

By Jesus' time, there was a rock formation known as the "gates of Hades" in this area that was believed to be a gateway to the underworld and a hot spot for demonic activities. Jesus brings about a cosmic confrontation at this very location in Matthew 16. Here, He challenges the authority of the lord of the dead and the entire underworld, essentially picking a fight with the realm of darkness as He proudly proclaims, "I am going to build my church and not one ounce of whatever power and authority you believe you have will prevail against My divine architecture."

Then what happens immediately after this is so profound: Jesus' transfiguration, which would've most likely been at the top of Mount Hermon since they were all talking at the base of this mountain just briefly before. Remember, this is the very place where the watchers "descended" to plot their plan of evil on the earth.

It's here that Jesus embodies the glory-essence of God. He is filled with Light. It is as if Jesus is shouting, "I am putting all hostile powers of the unseen world on notice. I have come to take back what is mine and share it with the sons and daughters of my Father. The Kingdom is at hand."

There is no power in the underworld that can overcome Jesus' authority. After all, they are under. We are seated with Christ above, partnering with Him to extend the Kingdom of Order within a world of disorder.

SPEAK UP: DECLARATION

I declare that Jesus has been given all authority in the heavens, the earth, and under the earth. I share in the spoils of His victory. Because of this, I have the honor of enforcing His victory and reveling in His triumph. I overcome through the blood of Jesus and the word of my testimony. There is no power in the underworld that can overcome my life. For it is no longer I that live, but Christ in me. What Jesus builds cannot be overtaken. I choose to co-labor with my brother, Jesus. The Kingdom will advance, the church will be built, and victory will extend.

THINK DEEP: MEDITATION

Revelation 12:11, Hebrews 2:14, Colossians 2:15, Matthew 16:17-19

Day 4: Before Time | In Time

We are to walk in the works that God prepared for us before time began (Ephesians 2:10). Everything that we are meant to be and release on this earth has already been completed in the heavenly realms, for God does not move gradually—He moved completely.

For example, Isaiah 53:5 states that "by His stripes we are healed." This, of course, was accomplished through the finished work of Christ. Through Him, healing has been fully established in the heavenly realms, and it now must be made manifest in the physical.

To take it one step further, keep in mind that the Lamb was slain before the foundations of the world (Revelation 13:8). This demonstrates that God moved completely in the heavenly realms before anything came into existence in the physical creation. When

WE ARRIVED HERE ON EARTH WITH ALL THAT WOULD BE REQUIRED FOR US TO ACHIEVE OUR DESTINY.

Jesus went to the cross 2,000 years ago, it was a physical manifestation of what had already taken place in the heavens. God always begins in the spiritual realms and then that which is completed begins to manifest in the physical realms.

Now, as Acts 17:28 states, we live, move, and have our being IN Him. Because God has already moved, we produce in time what was foreordained before time. 2 Timothy 1:9 says, God "saved us and called us to a holy calling, not because of our works but because of his own purpose and grace, which he gave us in Christ Jesus before the ages began." Think about this! God gave us everything we would ever need—purpose (who we are and what we are to release into the earth) and grace (the divine enablement to be and accomplish this)—before time began. We arrived here on the earth with all that would be required for us to achieve our destiny.

We should not strain, stress, or strive to make something happen. Weariness is not part of our inheritance; it is a fruit of the world. Everything that God has prepared for us is a gift, meaning it doesn't flow from our own efforts. It flows from our union. We are co-laboring. It is not simply up to us to fulfill what has been destined for our lives. This divine partnership is the space where things happen.

Speak Up: Declaration

I declare that God set aside amazing works for me before I had the capacity to dwell on them or participate in them. They have come from His heart for they are a gift from my Father. My Father's gifts don't come with stress, strain, or striving. I have the honor of allowing these works to unfold as I focus on our union. I have been given purpose, so I can know who I am and what I am called to do. I have been given grace, which empowers me to be who I am and do what I am called to do. I lack nothing to accomplish the unique and powerful call on my life. My Father doesn't move gradually, He has moved completely. Today I choose to move and have my being in Him.

Think Deep: Meditation

Ephesians 2:10, Isaiah 53:5, Revelation 13:8, Acts 17:28, 2 Timothy 1:9

Day 5: Meandering With Purpose

We tend to live and think in a linear fashion. When we consider a timeline, we think of it as having a beginning and an end. And when it comes to going through a course of action, we often opt for the shortest route possible.

This is not how God works. God is the beginning and the end simultaneously.

God, who always is, created all time, space, and energy. Since God doesn't exist within these limits, we cannot even begin to fathom the dimensionality of God. When we try to define God by these limits, we are attempting to describe Him from a human vantage point. We do this because it helps us to have a point of reference, but it cannot fully contain both the complexity and simplicity of who He is. Try imagining a place where time, space,

TRY IMAGINING A PLACE WHERE TIME, SPACE, AND ENERGY DON'T EXIST AND YET AT THE SAME TIME, CONTAINS ALL OF TIME, SPACE, AND ENERGY. THIS IS GOD'S SPACE.

and energy don't exist and yet at the same time, contains all time, space, and energy. This is God's space. If your head feels like it's going to explode, don't worry. Remember, the Holy Spirit has anointed you to know all things (1 John 2:20).

To that end, God is not constricted to think only in relation to time (a temporal mindset). He thinks in terms of the relationship and the journey to fulfilment (an eternal mindset).

Our linear thinking will not help us to fulfill who we are to be and what we are to release in the earth because it cannot commit our heart to the process. Our focus is usually the destination. His focus is the transformation. This involves meandering through the trails of life at the pace of grace. It's imperative that we set our minds on things above as we traverse these paths of breakthrough. Imagine yourself walking through a dense forest with a Father who wants nothing more than to be with you, show you the wonders of all you are, and unveil the beauty of what He has called you to unleash upon humanity.

If we are out of step with God, a word of prophecy from someone will not solve the problem. Obedience will. Personal prophecy, which is when God kindly reveals what He sees for us through another person, is an invitation to discover and align ourselves with the Father's view of us both in the present and the future. We must take action when words come our way. Think of prophecy as a partnership.

If we hear without doing, we are prone to delusion because we are continually forgetting what God has said and remembering what the enemy is saying.

Listen. Act. Enjoy the journey.

Speak Up: Declaration

My Father's focus is transformation. Thus, He loves to meander the trails of life with me. Time is working for the purposes of God in and through my life. He is not in a rush, for He is not bound by the constraints of time. I have become one with the beginning and the end, so I can trust my Father with the process. I don't need prophetic words to be the solutions for my life, but the confirmations of the solutions I have already been given in Christ. I have the honor of keeping pace with grace where I am walking out what has been foreordained before time began. I choose to listen. I choose to obey. I choose to enjoy the journey.

Think Deep: Meditation

Ephesians 2:10, 1 John 2:20, Revelation 22:13, James 1:22-25

Day 6: The Pattern of All Things

All philosophies end at the grave. In Christ, life begins at the grave. Living our lives is a mockery of death because we have been given His life. Thus, it's eternal. 1 Peter 1:23 (AMPC) says, "You have been regenerated (born again), not from a mortal origin (seed, sperm), but from one that is immortal by the ever living and lasting word of God."

God spoke, and this created a framework that established a pattern from His voice. This is the pattern of all things. Hebrews 11:3 says, "By faith we understand the universe was created by the word of God, so that what is seen was not made out of what was visible."

Every banana looks like a banana and every redwood tree looks like a redwood tree because the pattern sets the parameters for the formation of matter out of atoms. Every atom and every molecule has been framed up by the word of God and responds to His voice. Everything you see, even your own body, is a visible expression of its previously invisible existence.

Colossians 3:10 (MIR) says, "We stand fully identified in the new creation renewed in knowledge according to the pattern of the exact image of our Creator." We bear the pattern of the very image of God. We are the only part of the cosmos that carries this specific pattern, the source code for the exact image of Himself. We have become the revelation of the pattern He has revealed. We are a new creation that all of old creation is longing to see become what we have always been destined to be. It is time to identify and acquaint ourselves with the new.

We now have the honor of using our voice to speak from our oneness with God. This unified sound can cause an atmosphere to shift and situations to change. I remember a time when God instructed me to speak to the atmosphere of a city, specifically to declare that there would be a clearing. After doing this, up to 70 MPH winds that had not been forecasted began to blow. It's so vital for us to use our

> **LIVING OUR LIVES IS A MOCKERY OF DEATH BECAUSE WE HAVE BEEN GIVEN HIS LIFE.**

voices in unison with our Father and as we do, it begins to change the frequency of everything around us. Speak up. Speak out.

Speak Up: Declaration

I am a carrier of God's DNA. He has seeded me and I have been constructed from His voice. My life is the pattern of His image. I choose to identify and acquaint myself with the new. The old is gone and the new has come. When my Father speaks, creation comes forth. When I speak from our oneness, atmospheres shift, things begin to change, and the purposes of God are released. I am in a new world where I get to co-create with the architect of creation. I choose to use my voice just like my Father did and does. I will not be silent. I will not shut up nor be shut down.

Think Deep: Meditation

1 Peter 1:23, Hebrews 11:3, Colossians 3:10

Day 7: Guardians of the Galaxy

Angels are the true guardians of the galaxy. Psalm 91:11-12 says, "For he will command his angels concerning you to guard you in all your ways. On their hands they will bear you up, lest you strike your foot against a stone."

Angels protect our borders and oversee what comes in and what goes out. They have been commissioned to watch over us. Just as they hovered over each of the 120 in Acts 2:3 (the flame above each person), they hover over the heirs of Christ. They are the Heir Force.

Angels provide protection around all facets of our lives, guarding us from demonic intrusion. If you want to sense, see, or hear more of the angelic realm, then honor them. Honor helps us to see. For instance, if we

ANGELS ARE THE TRUE GUARDIANS OF THE GALAXY.

honor a person, we will see them more clearly as God sees them.

It is ridiculous to worship angels and equally as silly to ignore them. They have been assigned to us, to protect, minister, commission, and fulfill the words of God in and around our lives. They stick with us. How amazing is that?

Angels also love being involved in setting people free. Psalm 34:7 says, "The angel of the Lord encamps around those who fear him, and delivers them." "Delivers them" comes from the word chalats, of which one of the meanings is "to strip away." Angels can and will strip away bonds (spiritual and natural) to set people free. These include energetic bonds and emotional bonds, which are established through our agreements. As we break agreement with lies, angels can then start stripping away.

Chalats also means, "to draw out a victory, to rescue, or to bring forth a victory." I have personally partnered with angels in deliverance sessions to see bonds broken and it is always powerful. Angels are messengers that establish the dominion of King Jesus. They are greatly interested in performing the words of God such as John 8:36, "So if the Son sets you free, you will be free indeed."

Start declaring specific verses over yourself and your family, friends, home, work, church, neighborhood, city, and more, and you will give angels something to do.

SPEAK UP: DECLARATION

I have the guardians of the galaxy guarding my life. I am surrounded at all times on every side. The Heir Force doesn't even want me stubbing my toe against a stone. My Father has commissioned ministers of wind and flame to protect and minister to me. They love performing the words of God over my life. Thus, I choose to declare what my Father has said. Father, release Your hosts to help me walk in freedom, to accomplish what You have set before me, and bring me from heaven what I need to do these things.

THINK DEEP: MEDITATION

Psalm 91:11-12, Psalm 34:7, Psalm 103:20

Day 8: Kingdom Grounds

When you don't ground yourself in a spiritual community (spiritual family), this will lead to a flighty and uncommitted existence. In this space, deception can govern the self-imposed isolation and cause an inability to make Christ-conscious decisions.

This is because the Kingdom is primarily relational, not functional. Without relationships, there is no Kingdom. The Father, Son, and the Holy Spirit are not just the Trinity, they are a beautiful picture of family. Think about it like this: our earth has a biosphere and without it, life couldn't exist. The same goes for relationships and the Kingdom. Without relationships, there is no Kingdom. Thus, there is no life.

Jesus has chosen to co-labor with us rather than do everything Himself. How amazing that God not only saves us, but chooses to partner with us to see the fulfillment of His purposes in the earth? If Jesus has

> **A LACK OF FEEDBACK IN OUR LIVES WILL CREATE A SURPLUS OF POOR CHOICES.**

chosen relationship with us, then it's clear we need to choose relationships with others.

Without the iron that sharpens iron, our discernment will be dull. Rawthentic relationships come with tension (they sharpen, after all) and this very tension opens up our capacity to discern with a greater level of precision. No tension, no growth. A lack of feedback in our lives will create a surplus of poor choices. At times we need "in"-struction, which builds structure on the inside. This infrastructure will allow us to face difficulty, resistance, and pressure without being crushed. The people who can give us this feedback are like editors in our lives who can take our stories and make them better. I call this edit-ability.

Jesus said He would build His church, His body, in the earth. Why would we not want to participate and plug ourselves into a local expression of His architecture? Commit somewhere. Serve somewhere. Be a part of something bigger than yourself. Link arms with people who will help you live beyond just yourself.

Speak Up: Declaration

I declare that the Father, Son, and Holy Spirit are not

isolated from each other. They model community at all times. I have been woven into the most secure family in all of creation. This stability allows me the freedom to build community. I am not alone and I choose to not live life solo. I am powerful, so I can link arms with others who are powerful and together we will co-create with God. I am choosing to be a part of something bigger than myself. Jesus is committed to me, so I commit to His bride.

THINK DEEP: MEDITATION

1 Corinthians 3:9, Proverbs 1:3, Proverbs 16:20, Ephesians 5:25

DAY 9: MICROSCOPES AND MIRRORS

Just as microscopes help you magnify details and analyze, some people like to put their relationships under a microscope and micromanage. Critical and analytical, they meticulously examine the fault lines of the geography of every person around them, becoming experts in all things critical and analytical. This activity of insecurity is a self-protection modality that prohibits fertility. This kind of life will produce nothing of significance because it has nothing to do with life.

It's an empty life driven by fear, imprisoned to control, and expressed in manipulation. Our personal perception becomes our external projection. How we view ourselves will be projected on everyone around us. We have held our own lives hostage to a

> **WE LOVE OTHERS TO THE MEASURE OF THE LOVE WE HAVE ACCEPTED AND RECEIVED FOR OURSELVES.**

microscope that we can't help but use on others. Only when our sight aligns with the way our Father sees us, can we can then begin to project love, honor, and all the delicious fruits of the Holy Spirit.

Mirrors allow us to see ourselves for what we are. They prevent us from romanticizing our lives into something they are not. We can honestly assess our own fault lines as we gaze upon our own geography. Here, we can receive grace as it rains over us so we can reign in life. It is very powerful to see yourself and breathe in security that you are okay. In fact, when God made us, He said we were "very good."

We love others to the measure of the love we have accepted and received for ourselves. We cannot take people where we have refused to go. We cannot give away what we haven't received for ourselves. Corporate breakthrough begins with "my" breakthrough. A breakout of love through our lives begins with it overtaking our own. Love must flow outwards because it cannot be contained.

Perhaps we need to toss the microscopes to Goodwill and dust off a mirror. Our relationships will thank us.

Speak Up: Declaration

I declare I put down the microscope. I don't need to micromanage myself, or anyone else for that matter. I accept that I was loved before I even had the capacity to receive it. Love is freely flowing, and I freely bask in it for myself so I can allow its uncontainable nature to be released through me to others. Honesty and transparency are the hinges of my breakthrough. I choose to look in the mirror. I see myself today and know that I am a masterpiece of God. He is not willing to let me gloss over issues in my life. We can look in the mirror together. I am good enough. I am enough. My relationships are going to experience breakthrough because love is going to break out of me.

Think Deep: Meditation

John 13:34, Romans 13:12, Ephesians 5:2, James 1:22-24

Day 10: No Way Is There Gray

The foundation of confusion is the belief that there is a gray area.

When God set up creation, He divided the day and night. Light and dark. Genesis 1:5 says, "God called the light Day and the darkness he called Night. And there was evening and there was morning, the first day." This is a very clear distinction. All identity confusion, gender confusion, or any other type of confusion is a result of believing that light and dark blend, that there's a middle ground.

1 John 1:5-6 says, "God is light, and in him there is no darkness at all. If we say we have fellowship with him while we walk in darkness, we lie and do not practice the truth." God is pure light and emanates nothing else. He can only be who He is, which is

> **WE CAN HIDE WHO WE ARE IN THE PHYSICAL WORLD, BUT WE CANNOT HIDE WHO WE ARE IN THE HEAVENLY REALMS.**

Light. It is possible to walk in a constant state of clarity and stability since we are one with the very definition of clarity and stability. Even when things are shaken in our lives, our footing on a firm foundation keeps us secure.

In the physical world, life is in the blood (Leviticus 17). If your heart stops pumping blood, you cease to live. In the heavenly realms, life is in the light (John 1). We can hide who we are in the physical world, but we cannot hide who we are in the heavenly realms. The measure of light we walk in is in proportion to the light (truth) in our thought life. Light is a state of clarity, which means that when we don't have light in our thoughts, we will be confused. If we are confused about who we are in Him, we will have a difficult time being the light of the world.

As children of light, we are designed to shine brightly in a world desperate for clarity. We are the promised star seed spoken to Abraham of those who would be from above, outnumbering the stars in the sky. When we, His star seed, walk in the Light and think in the Light, we will model a clear focus so that others can see.

Speak Up: Declaration

I declare that I can discern what is in the Light and what is in the dark. Confusion is not in my identity and will not hinder my destiny. My Father IS Light, and I am in Him and He is in me. I cannot help but shine. I have the honor of walking in the Light, which means I live in a constant state of clarity. I declare any thoughts that are not found in the Light will be exposed. Today, I receive Your Light as it flows upon me, in me, and through me. Life is in the Light. My footing is firm and my clarity is strong. Thank you, Jesus, for coming as the Light!

Think Deep: Meditation

1 John 1:5-6, John 1:4, John 8:12, James 1:17

DAY 11: PIERCING AND PEACEFUL

There tends to be a belief in the church that when it comes to dealing with the demonic, we must be intensely rambunctious. Decibel levels, however, don't equal authority. The demonic realm doesn't respond to the volume level of someone's voice. They respond to authority.

God doesn't have hearing aids either. He has an incredible auditory range. It's interesting that when talking to some people, their decibel levels are normal in everyday conversations. Yet, when those same people get onstage at a ministry event, for example, they become different people. A casual conversation one moment turns into a yowling, frothy frenzy the next.

All this to say, some believe that being loud equals being spiritual. The higher the volume, the higher the spirituality.

THE DEMONIC REALM DOESN'T RESPOND TO THE VOLUME LEVEL OF SOMEONE'S VOICE. THEY RESPOND TO AUTHORITY.

Loud is great. I have some loud friends that are that way in any context. But when we think we have to be loud for God to move or the demonic to respond, we have lost our heavenly vantage point and the security of our identity. Jesus has commissioned us and given us His full authority. We have more than we need to see the demonic realm run for the hills and the Kingdom to advance without ceasing.

When it comes to worship, however, be loud. Shout praises to God. The body of Christ needs to open their mouths. Exuberant worship gets much more press in the Psalms than quiet and somber praise. There is a place for both, yet celebration seems to be more of a favorite to God.

The world is blind when the church is mute. We must use our voices. Let's be ourselves in that pursuit and let His authority be the expression of dominion. Also, let's rest in the authority He has given us and exercise it with a determined diligence, knowing that it's not the ear-splitting loudness that makes things happen.

Speak Up: Declaration

I have a voice and when I speak in the earth, God's voice can be heard. The demonic realm doesn't respond to my loudness, but to the bold authority with which I have been commissioned. Living my life is a mockery of darkness, so I choose to live life with the abundance Jesus has given me. My vantage point is high and my identity is deep. I am a son/daughter that can realize and actualize what has freely been given to me. What I have to say matters, so I am opening my mouth. My exuberant praise shifts atmospheres. I choose celebration over introspection.

Think Deep: Meditation

Psalm 98:4, Isaiah 44:23, John 3:31, Ephesians 1:21

DAY 12: UNITY VS. UNIFORMITY

If a church divides or, even worse, splits because of political viewpoints, then the guide of that church is a political spirit, not the Holy Spirit. This type of situation reveals the leaven upon which that community is feasting. In this case, it's the leaven of Herod.

The Holy Spirit will always gather diverse, multi-cultural, and multi-layered mindsets to form a unique body of believers that comes together around the presence of God in the midst of differences. It's a beautiful display of the power of unity, not uniformity. Psalm 133 says it's amazing when people dwell together in unity, and that God commands a blessing upon this type of Kingdom-centered synergy. Heaven is attracted to unity.

If we cannot be in relationships with people that have vastly different viewpoints from ours, then we are resting on the leaven of Herod and/or the Pharisee. The leaven of Herod is a political spirit, and the leaven of the Pharisee is a religious spirit. Each of these is driven by fear. They cause us to have a higher value for ideology rather than Christology.

TRUE LOVE SEES PAST OUR DIFFERENCES AND REMINDS US OF OUR SIMILARITIES.

We elevate temporal vantage points in place of the highest vantage point, which is being seated with Christ as one body.

The Holy Spirit desires integration among the diverse members of the body of Christ. When there is unity among different people and a colorful variety of complexity, it is a true sign and wonder to the world. John 13:35 says, "By this all people will know that you are my disciples, if you have love for one another." Notice that this verse isn't talking about our love for the world (it's a no-brainer that we extend His love to all), but rather it refers to our love for each other in Christ, and how clearly that demonstrates to the world what it means to be in Christ.

True love sees past differences and reminds us of our similarities.

Speak Up: Declaration

I declare that I am a part of a global network that is diverse, multi-cultural, and filled with multi-layered mindsets. The Holy Spirit is my helper and He is helping me dive into the beauty of unity. I reject any influence from the leaven of Herod or the leaven of the Pharisee that causes division, categorizing, shame, or guilt. I lay aside valuing ideology over Christology. I declare an increase of my capacity to love my own brothers and sisters in Christ. This will be a sign and a wonder to the world around me. I receive the flow of heaven coming upon me and the blessing of my Father in the midst of unity.

Think Deep: Meditation

Psalm 133:1-3, Mark 8:15, John 13:35

Day 13: Multi-Dimensional Space

We can find laboratory models of a space without time in two experiments called quantum tunneling and evanescent fields. Without going too much into the technical side of things, these are situations where wave packets bearing information cross a space without experiencing a lapse in time. This means that we can literally observe a window of eternity in a laboratory.

In Christ, we are eternal because we are one with Him. One of His names is Eternal One. In physical terms, eternity is multi-dimensional space. Eternity has space, but no time. Or at the very least, time works very differently from linear time and doesn't have the same limitations or restrictions.

IN CHRIST, WE ARE ETERNAL BECAUSE WE ARE ONE WITH HIM.

Being in Christ means we are multi-dimensional. Proverbs 20:27 says, "The spirit of man is the lamp of the LORD, Searching all the innermost parts of his being." Here, "innermost parts" means "bedroom or rooms," and "being" means "belly." Isn't this such a fascinating verse? To start, there are many "rooms" inside of us, as there is multi-dimensional space within us. Beyond that, our spirit is a light that God uses to search within us.

We can think of our spirit as electricity and our soul as a light bulb that contains the light and emanates that to our body. Our spirit sustains our soul, which sustains our body. As our minds are renewed, we are transformed (transfigured). This is the transfiguration of our flesh (DNA), so that every part of our existence (spirit, soul, and body) reflects light.

In John 14:2, Jesus says that He is going to His Father's house to prepare a place where there are many "rooms." We are the Father's house and inside of us is multi-dimensional space (eternity). Planes of existence. Realms of eternity. Jesus said that living waters would flow from our "belly." From our bellies flow rivers of living water that are not from this dimension.

It's awesome to know who we are in Christ. It is equally glorious to know what we are in Christ. We are new creatures in Christ that carry more than we can imagine within us, where Jesus Himself is preparing some incredible things.

Speak Up: Declaration

I declare that I have been made completely new in Christ. I am a new creation! I am a new creature in Christ! My wonderful Jesus is preparing a place inside of me where there are many rooms. I am one with Christ, so there is a world of complexity within me. He is using my spirit as a light to search the multi-dimensional space inside of me. Because there is so much inside, it must come outside. I declare His rivers are flowing all the time and that His love cannot be contained, it must be extended. I am His house where this extension can flow.

Think Deep: Meditation

Proverbs 20:27, John 7:38, John 14:2

Day 14: The Roars of the Lionesses

I remember being in a meeting where the topic of women preaching came up and a guy asked, "Is it right for women to stand behind pulpits and preach to a mixed audience?" My question in response was, "Is it right for men to stand behind pulpits and preach to a mixed audience? And what in the world is a pulpit—where in the New Testament do you see anyone standing behind a sacred piece of wood?"

I then asked if he and others allowed women to teach children in the churches they were leading. They replied, "Well, of course." I replied, "So, you allow women to teach at the most influential stage of life during which the majority of people's mindsets are being shaped? But, you won't allow women to teach those same people once they are grown up and their mindset patterns are established with the help of those very women?" The room was silent and the irony was as thick as Texas toast. Insecurity produces absurdity.

Augustine said, "But separately, as helpmate, the woman herself alone is not the image of God; whereas the man alone is the image of God as fully and completely as when the woman is joined with him." In this case, Augustine was listening to demons. In order for the image of God, the voice of God, and the nature of God to have full expression in the earth, both sexes must be present and functioning in authority. God is not just male. He made female in His image. Both masculine and feminine energy flow from Him.

> **WHEN ADAM WOKE UP, HE WASN'T JUST LOOKING AT HIS ALLY. HE WAS LOOKING AT HIS EQUAL.**

Adam had a wife within, and when he fell asleep, she came forth from his side. When Adam woke up, he wasn't just looking at his ally. He was looking at his equal. They would co-labor together to govern, subdue, and bring order to sacred space (the Garden). Jesus had a bride within and when He fell into the sleep of death on the cross, she came forth with water and blood as His side was pierced. A pure and spotless bride. We now co-labor with Jesus to govern, subdue, and bring order to the cosmos.

God is shaking the systems of the world and the church so that women can reclaim their voices of authority and God's voice can be expressed through their lives. Let the lionesses roar!

Speak Up: Declaration

I declare that God not only represents male but also female. He made both male and female in His image. Masculine and feminine energy flows from my Father. I declare women have a voice and carry an aspect of God that can only be clearly heard through His daughters. Father, break off any false mindset, insecurity, demonic theology, or anything else that would hinder your daughters from walking in Your authority and having a voice in the earth. I call out for the lionesses to rise and to roar in Jesus' name!

Think Deep: Meditation

Genesis 2:22, 1 Corinthians 11:11-12, John 19:34

DAY 15: DISCIPLESHIP 2.0

There is scientific evidence that if a single shaft of wheat is left undamaged and allowed to freely grow and reproduce, it would multiply in eight years into a crop large enough to feed the entire world population for an entire year.

We were never commanded to multiply churches. We were commanded to make disciples who reproduce and permeate throughout all of society. Much of what is currently called discipleship is actually abduction. When someone says yes to Jesus in church, we typically will abduct them from their natural spheres of influence and place them in a foreign environment where we train them beyond their level of obedience, placing expectation on them beyond their current capacity. This causes the person to become awkward with those in the world with whom they used to have effortless relationships.

> **THERE IS NOTHING PASSIVE ABOUT WHO WE ARE TO BE IN THIS WORLD.**

Also, because we have trained them beyond partnering with Jesus' vision, the Great Commission becomes the Great Omission, propelling people away from going into the world to advance the Kingdom. They adopt an underlying mindset that the world is dark, and that darkness has more power to influence us from the outside than the Light of the World inside.

Years ago at UC San Diego, where my wife and I currently do ministry, there was a large annual music festival on campus called the sun god festival. Our campus has an actual sun god statue. Our ministry decided to go and set up a booth to share words of knowledge and prophesy over people. I went to other Christian ministries to see if anyone else wanted to join. Some of the comments I received were, "But it's too dark of an environment for us to go into." What?! 1 John 4:4 says, "Little children, you are from God and have overcome them, for he who is in you is greater than he who is in the world."

By the way, we saw incredible fruit when we were at the sun god festivals. Many were touched by the love and power of God.

We are salt. We are light. We are yeast meant to influence the loaf from within. There is nothing passive about who we are to be in this world. We are not called to spectate, but to permeate. As long as a church service is viewed as the "main" event, there will be little done in the marketplace, which IS the main event. In Ezekiel 47 there is a picture of the temple and how the river got deeper the further it flowed from the temple.

The greatest miracles, signs, and wonders happen in the marketplace. Most of the miracles Jesus performed were there, and that is where He has called us to go.

Speak Up: Declaration

I declare that I am salt and I am light. Jesus has called me to not just participate but to permeate. What God has placed inside of me is to be reproduced and multiplied. All that is within cannot be contained, it must extend. I choose to co-labor with You, Jesus, and to follow Your river that flows and gets deeper as it rushes into the world. I embrace the marketplace as the main event and ask for a greater awareness of all that You have given me to do the works that You've prepared in advance. I am alive and the harvest is ripe.

Think Deep: Meditation

Ezekiel 47:1-12, Matthew 28:16-20, 1 John 4:4

DAY 16: THE DIVINE TRINE

There are limitations in trying to describe the Godhead. It's filled with so much complexity and simplicity at the same time. Human language falls short in finding the right words and analogies to provide understanding of this mysterious flow of Father, Son, and Holy Spirit. With that said, I will try my best to paint a picture to help us understand this transcendental dynamic.

Think of the trinity as the sun. The sun is, of course, the largest star in our solar system. It also contains more than 99.8 percent of the total mass of the solar system. Think of the sun as Father God. Then think of the light from the sun as Jesus, and the radiation (heat) from the sun as Holy Spirit.

The Father is the source of the Godhead. All things flow from Him. He always initiates and when He speaks, He always speaks the Word (Jesus). Now,

JESUS IS THE SHAPE-FORM AND VISIBILITY OF THE GODHEAD.

Jesus is the shape-form and visibility of the Godhead. God was bold enough to become flesh and be revealed in Jesus on the earth. Then, think of the Holy Spirit as emanations of energy from the Godhead. He is the presence of God in the earth and from Him flows the wondrous working power of God. This is not to say that the Holy Spirit is just some force or essence. God is one person that has three God-attributes. They have autonomy and, at the same time, function as a family from a place of union. Jesus said in John 10:30 that He and the Father were One.

The Father is the source outside of time, space, and energy. Jesus is the dimensions of the Father revealed within all time, space, and energy, and the Holy Spirit is the emanating energy throughout all of creation. God not only exists outside of all time, space, and energy, He also contains of all time, space, and energy.

Again, this is simply a description that cannot fully contain the complexity and simplicity of the communal dynamic of Father, Son, and Holy Spirit. What an amazing thing that God has chosen to reveal Himself in such a multi-layered way and at the same time is so approachable! He is not just a God who is far off wielding galaxies into existence, He chose to come to our level and become one of us (Jesus on the earth) so that we could become like Him.

Speak Up: Declaration

I declare that I am protected on all sides because the Father, Son, and Holy Spirit are in me and surround me. The Godhead models autonomy and family so well. I have been made one with them, so confidence becomes the consequence of oneness. I cannot help but be secure when the Father, Jesus, and the Holy Spirit are the epitome of stability and constancy. I declare my Father is good. I declare Jesus has fully revealed my Father. I declare the Holy Spirit teaches me all about and testifies of Jesus and reminds me that I am a child of God.

Think Deep: Meditation

John 10:30, Romans 8:16, 1 Corinthians 12:4-6, 2 Corinthians 13:14

DAY 17: THE SOURCE CODE

It's interesting that many will cry out for God to move and when He does, it's often upon a people group that is highly offensive to the ones crying out.

I believe God does this partly so that people's hearts will align with His and remain soft. This means that we can allow things to come our way without letting our biased thinking get in the way, so negativity doesn't take root and at the same time, our love for people doesn't diminish. This is crucial because some have hard eyes with which they look at people with a cynical bias and prejudice. This is where a person has come to a conclusion about someone before they understand the Father's heart for them. This is not an understanding at all, but rather a low-level thinking that has been influenced by scarcity narratives. This vantage point of lack comes from that person believing they themselves are not enough.

Our hearts and eyes need to be soft and our forehead hard.

God comes to offend these darkened perceptions and projections. He desires His kids to have soft eyes where they can see a person for who they really are. Honor helps us see clearly and love helps us impact deeply. Fear clouds our vision and lowers our ability to see properly.

God is going to do amazing things in people, and it will most likely begin with those that represent the highest level of offense. Remember, it's all about grace. When we delve into the depths of grace, we will find places that will confront our lack of understanding of the beautiful nature of grace. It reveals how much we think we were responsible for grace coming to us.

OUR FATHER IS THE VERY SOURCE CODE THAT WILL HELP US REFRAME AND RECODE OUR EYES FROM HARD TO SOFT.

Don't allow the media, the church, or any other institution form your internal narrative and cause you to solidify a faulty perspective of anyone. Our Father is the very Source code that will help us reframe and recode our eyes from hard to soft. This is imperative for us to know what the Father is doing and how to move forward with His purposes in the earth.

SPEAK UP: DECLARATION

I declare that I can see because I have been given eyes to have a clear perspective. To the eyes of my heart I say, "Let there be Light!" My Father is Light; thus, He is clarity. I am a child of Light; thus, I am filled with clarity. Jesus, help me to see how You saw everyone around You from the frame of reference of Truth. I reject any darkened perceptions and projections. I embrace the softness of my Father's eyes and the flow of grace to offend my mindsets if needed.

THINK DEEP: MEDITATION

John 5:19, Romans 12:10, Ephesians 1:18, 1 Peter 2:17

Day 18: Fruitful Intoxication

One must assess a tree by its fruit. Let your life that's connected to the Vine produce delicious and vibrant Kingdom fruits. To that end, I want to encourage anyone that has had accusations come against them. Don't allow yourself to stoop to a low level and eat the spoiled fruits of disappointment and resentment.

Jesus allowed Himself to be crushed so that we could be whole. His brokenness became our completeness. We have the high honor of tasting His goodness when accusations come our way. Being connected to the Vine means there are lots of big grapes, which when crushed become bottles of incredibly delicious wine. Love wine, to be exact. When others want to crush you, it is a great opportunity to produce wine. Jesus said in Matthew

> **WE HAVE THE HIGH HONOR OF TASTING HIS GOODNESS WHEN ACCUSATIONS COME OUR WAY.**

5:11 that we are blessed when people insult, persecute, and falsely say things about us. Every time we experience this, it's an opportunity for a bounty of blessing to bounce into our lives.

Song of Songs 2:4 shows us that Jesus has a house of wine. I believe this is a special place for moments in our lives where we face accusation, persecution, and more. Imagine Jesus pulling down a bottle that was made in the year of your struggle. He then begins to pour out new wine for a new season from all the crushing of the past season. He uses all things for good.

Allow yourself to be intoxicated by His love in these times and then it will flow in all directions, including to those who have accused you. The fragrance of Christ will be billowing upward and outward wherever you go. This euphoria will cause you to be in a state of generosity where you can't wait to give away forgiveness and declare blessings on those who have hurt you.

A person who does not acknowledge the fruit of another individual's life is like a person trying to convince someone else that water is not wet. We don't have to try to prove or defend ourselves when we are lost in the exhilaration of our first love with Him. When our priority is our first love, then there will be love for every last one.

The Vine is always producing fruit. We are the branches, which means it is our responsibility to bear the fruit that the Vine produces. His fruit hangs on our lives. Jesus is a Kingdom farmer's market that always has the freshest and most abundant fruits around. As we abide in the awareness of our oneness, fruit will naturally grow and love will powerfully flow.

Speak Up: Declaration

I declare that I am connected to the Vine and He produces fruit. I have the honor of bearing the fruit that Jesus is producing. For every accusation, moment of persecution, and false piece of information about me, there is an infinite supply of love. I get to freely give away what I have freely received. I am blessed when I am accused. I am blessed when I am persecuted. I am blessed when people say false things about me. I choose to allow myself to be intoxicated by the love wine of Jesus. As others try to crush who I am, wine is being made that will supply a beautiful flow of the fruitfulness of my life.

Think Deep: Meditation

Matthew 5:11-12, John 5:4-5, Acts 5:41, 1 Peter 4:14

DAY 19: SETTLING

Do you know the name of Abraham's father, without doing a Google search or scouring through your Bible? Probably not. Only a small handful of verses reference him. His name was Terah, which means "wanderer." In Genesis 11, he was headed toward the promise land but then chose to settle in Haran, which means "mountainous." Think about this: he is en route to the land of promise but decides to settle in a valley among mountains.

When faced with mountains, we will either settle before them or move them. If we settle, very little will be written about our lives. Hence, not much is said of Terah and the details of his life. This may be because few details of his life were worth recording.

What seems reasonable to us may actually be a product of fear. Fear lowers a person's ability in all areas of life, including the ability to advance. A

> **A RATIONAL MIND ALWAYS SETTLE FOR LESS AND UNBELIEF IS EASILY ACCESSIBLE FROM A PLACE OF REASON.**

rational mind always settles for less and unbelief is easily accessible from a place of reason. It's not that God is unreasonable, He is just trans-rational.

To settle is to have only one generation in mind. Abram chose to take a step of faith and leave Haran, and his step caused a ripple effect to flow through time. Romans 4:16 states that Abraham is the spiritual father of faith. His choice to obey without knowing the way is still being experienced today.

When we are abide in the world, we abide in things that are not worthwhile. This settlement will do nothing to help us live out our destiny. Confidence is the consequence of oneness in Jesus. We will be overwhelmed by situations in life unless we become consumed by who God is for us. Rejoicing refreshes our thinking and ushers in a superior atmosphere that is electric with faith and boldness. It is here that our sight rises to our position in Christ.

We must open our mouths and speak to the atmosphere and any mountain about who our Father is for us. Adam lost his crown in the garden because he listened when he should've spoken. Ecclesiastes 8:4 says, "The word of the king has power." Kings exercise their dominion primarily by speaking. Silence is agreement.

Speak up and declare out, then mountains will begin to move. Jesus said in Matthew 17:20 that if we had faith even the size of a mustard seed that we could speak to the mountain and it would move. Notice Jesus didn't say to speak to Him about the mountain. We must use our voice and speak up!

SPEAK UP: DECLARATION

I choose to speak up and declare out. The word of the king has power, so I am going to use words. I am a king in my Jesus, who is the King of kings. I will not settle, for I have dreams that cannot be contained in a valley. Anywhere outside the enjoyment of God is dry and I live for the enjoyment of God. My destiny requires me to move forward and upward. To all the mountains in my life, I declare that you will begin to move. I allow myself to become consumed with who my Father is for me. I rejoice and dance before the mountains in my life. Let me tell you about my Father and how much He provides for me. I will no longer be silent!

THINK DEEP: MEDITATION

Genesis 11:31, Ecclesiastes 8:4, Matthew 17:20, Romans 4:16

DAY 20: HOLY HELP

The Holy Spirit was sent as our helper, not our servant. This means we cannot possibly think we can do life on our own. No person is self-made. That's an illusion.

At the same time, we shouldn't believe that we don't have to take responsibility or do our best simply because we have God and the Heir Force (angels). Those who live their lives thinking they just need to rely on God and not do anything won't receive much help. Holy Spirit is our HELPER. We must realize we are responsible to exercise our free will to partner with God's heart and original intent for our lives. Jesus has chosen to link up with us to co-labor for His full reward.

Think of it this way. The forward motion of our planet causes a centrifugal force (moving away from a center) and the gravitational pull of the sun causes a centripetal force (moving toward a center). Both forces work in harmony to establish a stable orbit of our planet around the sun. Our free will exercises a centrifugal force while what's been foreordained for our lives exercises a centripetal force over human life.

Ephesians 2:10 says, "For we are his workmanship, created in Christ Jesus for good works, which God prepared beforehand, that we should walk in them." If there isn't a centrifugal force, the earth would crash into the sun. If we don't exercise free will, works prepared in advance are of no benefit to our lives. If there's no centripetal force, the earth would be thrown into the darkness of space. By failing to walk out what was foreordained for us, our lives would be thrown into darkness.

WE MUST REALIZE WE ARE RESPONSIBLE TO EXERCISE OUR FREE WILL TO PARTNER WITH GOD'S HEART AND ORIGINAL INTENT FOR OUR LIVES.

It's important to understand that more effort isn't the answer. More effort without wisdom (the application of revelation) produces fatigue and weariness. Jesus sends out an invitation saying, "Come to me, all who are weary and burdened, and I will give you rest." This wasn't an invitation to a day spa where we take a nap in a lavender-scented hammock. It's to partner, align, and participate in the Kingdom of Order. It's to resist our self-interest, self-sufficiency, and self-reliance. Here we find stability and security in the midst of disharmony.

His song of harmony (order) plays as we dance the dance of affinity. From this place, we can then release His order into a world of discord, distortion, and disorganization as we pass out invitations to the very place of rest we have found in Christ.

SPEAK UP: DECLARATION

I declare that I need help. If Jesus said He cannot do anything apart from the Father, then I come into agreement with Him and recognize my need for assistance. I declare that I am one with You God, so I don't have any fear of being apart from You. Thank You for the works that You prepared before creation. I choose to walk into all that You have destined me to release into the earth. Jesus, give me a greater awareness of the rest that I can find in You. I reject self-sufficiency and self-reliance. I get to co-labor with my beautiful Jesus with the help of the Holy Spirit and the Heir Force. I declare that the order of the Kingdom will be released through my life as I exercise my free will and live out the works prepared in advance for me.

THINK DEEP: MEDITATION

Matthew 11:28, John 14:26, 1 Corinthians 3:9, Ephesians 2:10

DAY 21: THE FREQUENCY OF OLD AND NEW CREATION

Colossians 1:16-17 says, "For by him all things were created, in heaven and on earth, visible and invisible, whether thrones or dominions or rulers or authorities—all things were created through him and for him. And he is before all things, and in him all things hold together."

John 1:3 says, "All things were made through him, and without him was not any thing made that was made."

Without Jesus, nothing visible or invisible would exist. Everything resides within Jesus, both unseen and seen, because without Him, nothing has substance or form. Jesus is the song of love the Father sang over creation. He is the frequency of love. God declared, or sang, in the beginning, "Let there be light." Notice that God spoke in present tense. The Father was releasing His full bandwidth of glory onto a blank canvas through Jesus.

The Father was illuminating the cosmos with the glory of Jesus. He is the light of the world (John 8:12). He is the lamp of the heavens (Revelation 21:23). The light that was is the light that is: Jesus. The Father imparted form and substance into a once dark, formless canvas. All things came into existence through Jesus. The mysteries of the cosmos are available to those who explore their new zip code in Christ. The glory of God in Jesus is the energy within all life, while matter is the physical demonstration of His spiritual substance. By the way, without light, nothing would be held together as light is the only transitioning agent that brings the non-local (unseen) into the local (seen). Jesus is the transition, heaven coming to earth.

> **JESUS IS THE SONG OF LOVE THE FATHER SANG OVER CREATION. HE IS THE FREQUENCY OF LOVE.**

Before creation, the Holy Spirit brooded (vibrated) over the waters. Then creation began when the Father sang let there be light, revealing Jesus as all things came into existence through Him—the one who holds it all together.

Similarly, our physical bodies are primarily comprised

of water, and the Holy Spirit broods (vibrates) over the waters of our lives as in old creation. When we become a new creation, the Father sings over us (Zephaniah 3:17) and His voice is like many waters (Revelation 14:2) resonating within us at the very vibrational frequency of His love and glory. We are called to be the light of the world (Matthew 5:14). Sound familiar? God had said "let there be light," and we are light.

We are the only part of creation that is new. All of old creation groans for new creation to be revealed. We are in Christ, which means we are in the very song of the Father, living from the frequency of His glory. It is called harmony. It is called destiny. It is called eternity. We have become the revelation of the pattern He has revealed.

The more we know who we are and what we are in Christ, the more His song can flow through our lives, spilling into all of creation. We need spiritual substance outside of our physical existence. Jesus is the substance. He is the shape-form of the Father.

We are born into darkness to see the light, to walk in the light, to become a reflection of the light, and to finally become light. We have become children of light in a Kingdom of Light. We were created to shine.

SPEAK UP: DECLARATION

I declare that all things visible and invisible came into existence because of Jesus. He is the beginning and the end. He is the true image of the invisible God.

He is the firstborn of creation. He is before all things. In Him all things are held together. He is the head of the church and the firstborn from the dead. Through Him all things are reconciled to God. I attain peace through His blood. Once I was alienated, but now I am reconciled. Jesus is substance. He is form. I am one with Jesus. I am a new creation. I have become light. I am a child of light in a Kingdom of Light.

THINK DEEP: MEDITATION

Matthew 5:14, John 1:3, John 8:12, Colossians 1:16-17, Revelation 21:23

About the Author:

I have always been a dreamer, looking to the horizon and knowing there is more. I wasn't content with boxes when I knew I could fly. At the age of 17 I fully committed my life to Jesus. Through my relationship with Him, I have become even MORE of a dreamer. He said ALL things are possible to those who BELIEVE.

Playing it safe is risky, so instead I have lived my life as a risk-taker. Almost everything I have done in my life has involved stepping out in faith and expecting something good to come out of it. I am a spiritual entrepreneur that can see the horizon and take leaps of faith to get there.

At times I have doubted, second-guessed, and fallen flat on my face. Yet, I have learned God loves and rewards risk. There is something exhilarating and frightening about stepping into the unknown, certain only of my trust in God, who has proven Himself time and time again as trustworthy and faithful.

Now, over two decades after committing myself to Jesus, I am still risking and believing for the impossible. I am passionate about helping others see the greatness God has deposited in them and become more aware of their co-ascension with Christ. I love seeing people have God encounters that break off limitations, low-level thinking, and powerless living.

I wear a myriad of hats in my life: husband, father, spiritual father, son, pastor, author, provoker, consultant, and friend. For the past 20 years, I have sown many seeds into secular universities, doing campus ministry. Currently, my family and I are bringing the Kingdom to UC San Diego in beautiful San Diego, California. I enjoy living my life with my wife, Cecilee, and our two amazing children, Eowyn and Liam.

Brian's Resources

BOOKS

Jumpstart

Little Beans and
a Big God

The Ascended Life

Remember When

PODCAST

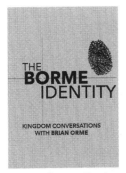

Borme Identity Podcast
iborme.com/podcasts

E-COURSE

Mindset Legacy E-Course
iborme.com/getcourse

 Find these and other great resources at: iborme.com

Stay Connected

 website   *iborme.com*

facebook   *facebook.com/borme*

twitter   *@blondboybrian*

instagram   *@borme*

youtube   *youtube.com/kingdomstrate*

linkedin   *Brian Orme*

For more information
iborme.com/about/speaking

join the mailing list

Request Brian to Speak

STUDENTS + CHURCHES + CONFERENCES

FOR
Retreats, conferences, one-night gatherings,
churches, leadership events